The Narrative Rosary

"God, the inspirer and author of both Testaments, wisely arranged that the New Testament be hidden in the Old Testament and the Old Testament be made manifest in the New Testament."
Dei Verbum (DV16)

By

Charles M. Urban, Sr., M.S. Ed.

NIHIL OBSTAT:
Brian D. Chadwick

IMPRIMATUR:
Most Reverend Dale J. Melczek
Bishop of Gary
February 28, 2006

The *Nihil Obstat* and *Imprimatur* are official declarations that a book or pamphlet is free of doctrinal or moral error. No implication is contained therein that those who have granted the *Nihil Obstat* and *Imprimatur* agree with the contents, opinions, or statements expressed.

Special Thanks to:
Rev. Derrick F. Dudash
St. Helen Catholic Church
Hebron, Indiana

Acknowledgements

Scripture excerpts from the *New American Bible with Revised New Testament and Psalms* Copyright © 1991, 1986, 1970 by the Confraternity of Christian Doctrine, Washington, D.C. Used with permission. All Rights Reserved. No part of the *New American Bible* may be reproduced in any form without permission in writing from the copyright owner.

English translation of the *Catechism of the Catholic Church* for the United States of America Copyright © 1994, United States Conference of Catholic Bishops—Libreria Editrice Vaticana. English translation of the *Catechism of the Catholic Church*: *Modifications from the "Editio Typica"* Copyright © 1997, United States Catholic Conference of Catholic Bishops—Libreria Editrice Vaticana. Used with permission.

TABLE OF CONTENTS

The Sorrowful Mysteries

The Glorious Mysteries

Introduction

When we pray the Rosary, we petition and invoke the Virgin Mary, as the mother of Our Lord, as "our mother," which she became at the foot of the cross by her Son's command, to spiritually intercede in our daily rosary prayer life to bring us into a close and holy relationship with her Son, Jesus.

Throughout the course of our lives, many of us have had favors and graces granted to us through our Blessed Mother's intercession. After all, was there ever a request that she made of her Son that Jesus did not fulfill?

There is not much said in the Scriptures about Mary and Joseph and "all" they did because the focus of the Gospels is about Our Lord, His saving work, His suffering, His salvific act and Resurrection.

However, one can only reasonably conclude, even without reading or informing oneself about what the early Church Fathers taught and wrote about Mary, her role as Mother of God, and her subsequent role in the Church, that Mary's purpose in the Church has "always" been one of mothering Her "spiritual" children to come to a relationship with her Son, Jesus.

There is no place in Holy Scriptures that speaks about Mary's Assumption (being assumed, or taken up, body and soul) into Heaven, or her Coronation as Queen of Heaven. This is an understanding of Mary's role as Mother of Jesus and Mother of God.

As Jesus hung on the cross between the two criminals, the first one chides Christ to come off the cross. The second criminal admits that they deserve their punishment.

At this point the second criminal "confesses" that Jesus has done nothing wrong and does not deserve the punishment as do the two of them.

The second criminal now goes beyond admitting his guilt and Jesus' innocence; he asks Jesus to remember him when Jesus enters His reign and he acknowledges Jesus to be the Messiah by making such a request.

Jesus then says to him: . . . "Amen, I say to you, today you will be with me in Paradise." (Lk 23:43)[1] Jesus did not say "some day," or "on the last day," He said: "TODAY!"

Amidst Jesus' unendurable pain and intolerable agony, the second thief is crowned the church's first saint and becomes the vindication for "all" His suffering for He would have endured it all if only for this one single sinner.

What does this have to do with Mary's Assumption into heaven body and soul, or her Coronation as Queen of Heaven?

If Jesus promised a thief "paradise the same day" of his death, how much more would Our Lord do for His own mother? He would! And, He did!

---

1. *Saint Joseph Edition of the NEW AMERICAN BIBLE*, Revised New Testament of the *New American Bible* © 1986 Confraternity of Christian Doctrine (CCD). Washington, D.C.

Fr. Hardon's *Modern Catholic Dictionary* defines Mary's Assumption because of the following: ". . . she was full of grace and remained preserved from the consequence of sin, namely corruption of the body after death and postponement of bodily happiness in heaven until the last day"[2] There is no doubt that He would and He did just that for His own mother.

In the Book of Genesis we read of the "assumption of Enoch" how Enoch walked with God, and he was no longer here, for God took him. (Gn 5:24)

This is additionally referenced in the Book of Wisdom which says of him:
> He who pleased God was loved;
> he who lived among sinners was
> transported. (Wis 4:10)

In the chapter concerning the Death and Burial of Moses it states that: "and he was buried in the ravine opposite Beth-peor in the land of Moab, but to this day no one knows the place of his burial." (Dt 34:6)

In Fr. McKenzie's *Dictionary of the Bible,* it states that: "The apocryphal book of *Jubilees* was attributed to Moses. His powers as wonder worker were enhanced in legend; in particular the wonders of his death and burial were elaborated, as in the apocryphal *Assumption of Moses*."[3]

---

2. Modern Catholic Dictionary. John A. Hardon, S.J., Doubleday & Company, Inc. 1980. See: *"Assumption"*: Page 45.
3. McKenzie, John L. S.J. *Dictionary of the Bible*. New York, N.Y. McMillan Publishing Company. 1965. Page 590.

Then, there is the passage that describes the prophet Elijah being assumed into heaven by a flaming chariot. (See 2 Kgs 2:11).

Jesus took Peter, James, and John to Mount Tabor where He was transfigured before their eyes, and suddenly Moses and Elijah appeared to them . . . (See Mt 17:1-3)

If God can assume Enoch and Elijah into heaven before their physical deaths, if Jesus could raise from the dead Lazarus (Jn 11:44), the widow's son at Naim (Lk 7:11-17), Jairus' daughter (Mk 5:21-43), and His own resurrection (Mt 28:1-20),[4] if God can make Moses and Elijah appear on Mount Tabor, and if the Angel Gabriel was sent to announce to Mary that she would conceive and bear a son by the power of the Holy Spirit, can we doubt that when Jesus tells his beloved disciple, John, at the foot of the cross to behold Mary as his mother, and then assigns his mother to become the mother of St. John, that He did not also infer that she was to become our mother, and we her children?

Do we not call each other brothers and sisters in Christ, or in the Lord?

Can one then intellectually deny that He had no other explicit intent or divine purpose in mind?

So, we now come to the purpose of these meditations on the Rosary.

4. Wijngaards, John. *Handbook on the Gospels*. Ann Arbor, Michigan. Servant Books. 1979. Page 200.

The new *Catechism of the Catholic Church*,[5] states that:
The Church "forcefully and specifically exhorts all the
Christian faithful . . . to learn 'the surpassing knowledge of
Jesus Christ,' by frequent reading of the divine Scriptures.
'Ignorance of the Scriptures is ignorance of Christ.'"[6]

Because the text of "this book" is written in narrative
style, it is hoped to recall some, obviously not all, pertinent
events of Our Lord's life in chronological order to facilitate
the reader to later recall the mysteries of the Rosary in story
form and consequently press on to a more complete scrip-
tural knowledge of Jesus.

Rather than to enumerate on the life of Christ here, allow
the selected texts to reveal to you all His glory which He
enjoys as King of Kings, Lord of Lords, and Host of Hosts.

Pray it often enough and Christ's Paschal Mystery will
unfold both in the Old and the New Testaments verses, and
in the teachings of our Catholic Faith.

As one of my Theology professors stated many years ago:
**"The New Testament is hidden in the Old Testament, and
the Old Testament is revealed in the New Testament."**

My fervent prayer in locating the appropriate
corresponding texts is that none of the biblical texts used

---

5. *Catechism of the Catholic Church*. Copyright © 1994 by the United
States Catholic Conference, Inc. – Libreria Editrice Vaticana. Article
133.
6. Cf. DV25, cf.*Phil* 3:8 and St. Jerome, *Commentariorum in Isaiam libri
xviii* ptol.:PL 24, 17b.

in this book are inappropriately attributed to the verses selected for each of the meditations; and can only request your leniency at a layman's attempt to make possible the appropriate connections from the New Testament to the Old New Testament meditations on these mysteries of the Holy Rosary.

God destined from the moment of the Fall that Mary, would be conceived full of grace, divinely fecundated[7] by His Holy Spirit, and become the Ark of His New Covenant, His Son, the Word made flesh, Our Lord and Savior, Jesus Christ, to ransom mankind from the stain of the garden by the forgiveness of sins.

Finally, "He [the holy Spirit] *makes present* the mystery of Christ, supremely in the Eucharist, in order to reconcile them, to *bring them into communion* with God, that they may 'bear much fruit.' "[8 & 9]

---

7. cf. *Catechism of the Catholic Church*. Article 485.
8. Cf. *Jn* 15:8, 16.
9. cf. *Catechism of the Catholic Church*. Article 737.

A Daily Rosary Offering Prayer

O Most Sacred Heart of Jesus, through the Immaculate Heart of Mary, I (we) offer you these next five decades of the Rosary:

For all the intentions of the Immaculate of Mary for this month.
For our Holy Father and for our holy Mother Church.
For all those who hold and teach the Catholic faith handed down from the Apostles.
For an increase in vocations.
For the holy souls in purgatory.
For the conversion of sinners and the world.
For a just and lasting peace.
For all our family members, our friends, and our foes.
For all those who are separated from us through death, distance, or divorce.
For the strength, the courage, the wisdom, and the success with which to perform our daily duties.
For all those who suffer from homelessness, hunger, ill health, and unemployment.
For all those children who suffer from abuse, abortions, abandonment, and neglect.
For our parish and diocesan family, especially for those whom we have been asked to pray for, those who have asked us to pray for them, those who are in need, and those whom we have promised to pray for.
For the parish pastor and other parish priests, and all previous priests who have taught us, guided us, befriended us, and have given us the sacraments of baptism, reconciliation, and most especially the Eucharist.
For our Bishop and all Bishops and Cardinals.

For all religious: missionaries, sisters, brothers, transitional and permanent deacons, seminarians, novices, and for all those who continue Your work in religious or lay ministries that they may receive the necessary graces for their state of life and the strength of mind, body, and will to perform their daily duties competently.

For all world and government leaders, especially our President, that they may all acknowledge You as Creator and govern according to Your justice and compassion especially toward the elderly, the poor, the disadvantaged, the homeless, the infirm, the disabled, the unemployed, those who are underemployed, heads of household, the family, the children, and the unborn.

And finally, for those who serve to protect us: our health workers, those who supply us with food, shelter, and clothing, our firemen, our policemen, and our soldiers.

How to Pray This Rosary

Everyone has heard the familiar quote that "a family that prays together stays together," and during these trying times in our society for parents and children, one can not help but think that prayer should be an inclusive and mandatory participation for all its members.

As an elementary classroom teacher I knew that the children did not want to hear me read to them constantly, nor did I have the voice to do so continuously. Besides, that would soon become boring!

One way to involve all the members of your family is to assign different meditations to a particular group.

For instance, may I suggest that one parent read the Catechism of the Catholic Church's (CCC) meditation after saying the Our Father prayer, while the second parent could read the New Testament (NT) meditation after saying the Hail Mary, and assign the children to read the Old Testament (OT) Meditation.

Another possibility is for both parents to simultaneously read the CCC meditation after reciting the Our Father, and assign the NT Meditation to the girls and the OT Meditation to the boys, or vice a versa, after reciting the Hail Mary.

There is a triple benefit in including the children in the prayers.

First, children love to be shown respect, allowed to participate in adult events, and are more than willing to accept meaningful responsibility.

Next, by involving them in a controlled manner, they are learning that sharing is part of their responsibility toward each other and is a great confidence and character builder.

Finally, by assigning the children a larger participation in the reading process, you may be able to detect any reading "miscues" your child, or children, are performing. That is, words which are being mispronounced, words that the child may not be familiar with and can be helped at a later time to add these to their vocabulary repertoire, detect a possible speech impediment that may not have been otherwise noticed, and many other possible clues.

Consequently, it must be said that besides the growth in your own family's spirituality, there are also practical benefits and advantages to praying together.

Prayers

The Apostles' Creed

I believe in God, the Father Almighty, Creator of heaven and earth; and in Jesus Christ, His only Son, Our Lord, Who was conceived by the Holy Spirit, born of the Virgin Mary, suffered under Pontius Pilate, was crucified, died, and was buried. He descended into hell; the third day He rose again from the dead; He ascended into heaven, sits at the right hand of God, the Father Almighty; from thence He shall come to judge the living and the dead. I believe in the Holy Spirit, the holy Catholic Church, the communion of Saints, the forgiveness of sins, the resurrection of the body, and life everlasting. Amen.

Our Father

Our Father, who Art in heaven, hallowed be Thy Name; Thy kingdom come, Thy will be done on earth as it is in heaven. Give us this day our daily bread and forgive us our trespasses as we forgive those who trespass against us, and lead us not into temptation, but deliver us from evil. Amen.

Hail Mary

Hail Mary full of grace, the Lord is with you, blessed are you among women, and blessed is the fruit of your womb, Jesus. Holy Mary, Mother of God, pray for us sinners now and at the hour of our death. Amen.

Glory To The Father

Glory be to the Father, and to the Son, and to the Holy Spirit. As it was in the beginning, is now, and ever shall be, world without end. Amen.

Fatima Prayer

Oh! my Jesus, forgive us our sins, save us from the fires of hell and lead all souls to heaven, especially those in most need of Thy mercy.

Hail Holy Queen

Hail, Holy Queen, Mother of Mercy; our life, our sweetness, and our hope. To you do we cry poor banished children of Eve. To you do we send up our sighs, mourning and weeping in this valley of tears. Turn then, most gracious Advocate, your eyes of mercy towards us. And after this exile, show unto us the blessed fruit of your womb, Jesus. O Clement, O Loving, O Sweet Virgin Mary.

V. Pray for us, O holy Mother of God.

R. That we may be made worthy of the promises of Christ.

St. Michael the Archangel

St. Michael the Archangel, defend us in the day of battle, be our protection against the wickedness and snares of the Devil. May God rebuke him, we humbly pray, and do thou, Prince of the Heavenly Host, by the power of God, thrust into hell Satan, and all the other evil spirits who prowl through the world seeking the ruin of souls. Amen.

The
Joyful
Mysteries

The Annunciation

Our Father

Angels have been present since creation and throughout the history of salvation, announcing this salvation from afar or near and serving the accomplishment of the divine plan: they closed the earthly paradise; protected Lot; saved Hagar and her child; stayed Abraham's hand; communicated the law by their ministry; led the People of God; announced births and callings; and assisted the prophets, just to cite a few examples.[10] Finally, the angel Gabriel announced the birth of the Precursor and that of Jesus himself.[11 & 12]

---

10. Cf. *Job* 38:7 (where angels are called "sons of God"); *Gen* 3:24; 19; 21:27; 22:11; *Acts* 7:53; *Ex* 23:20-23; *Judg* 13; 6:11-24; *Isa* 6:6; *1 Kings* 19:5.
11. Cf. *Lk* 1:11-16.
12. *Catechism of the Catholic Church*. Article 332.

Hail Mary

1 - **NT Meditation**: In the days of Herod, King of Judea, there was a priest named Zechariah of the priestly division of Abijah; his wife was from the daughters of Aaron, and her name was Elizabeth. Both were righteous in the eyes of God, observing all the commandments and ordinances of the Lord blamelessly. But they had no child, because Elizabeth was barren and both were advanced in years. (Lk 1:5-7)

1 - **OT Meditation**: . . . the eighth to Abijah . . . but a double portion to Hannah because he loved her, though the LORD had made her barren. (1 Chr 24:10; 1 Sam 1:5)

Hail Mary

2 - **NT Meditation**: the angel of the Lord appeared to him, standing at the right of the altar of incense. Zechariah was troubled by what he saw, and fear came upon him. But the angel said to him, "Do not be afraid, . . .Your wife Elizabeth will bear you a son, and you shall name him John . . . for he will be great in the sight of [the] Lord. He will drink neither wine nor strong drink. He will be filled with the holy Spirit even from his mother's womb, . . ." (Lk 1:11 . . . 15)

2 - **OT Meditation**: "Speak to the Israelites and tell them: When a man (or a woman) solemnly takes the nazirite vow to dedicate himself to the LORD, he shall abstain from wine and strong drink; . . ." (Num 6:2-3a)

Hail Mary

3 - **NT Meditation**: ". . . and he will turn many of the children of Israel to the Lord their God. He will go before him in the spirit and power of Elijah to turn the hearts of fathers toward children and the disobedient to the understanding of the righteous, to prepare a people fit for the Lord." (Lk 1:16-17)

3 - **OT Meditation**:

Lo, I will send you
    Elijah, the prophet,
Before the day of the LORD comes,
    the great and terrible day,
To turn the hearts of the fathers to their children,
    and the hearts of the children to their fathers
Lest I come and strike
    the land with doom. (Mal 3:23-24)

Hail Mary

4 - **NT Meditation**: Then Zechariah said to the angel, "How shall I know this? For I am an old man, and my wife is advanced in years." And the angel said to him in reply, "I am Gabriel, who stand before God. I was sent to speak to you and to announce to you this good news." (Lk 1:18-19)

4 - **OT Meditation**:

As high as the heavens are above the earth,
    so high are my ways above your ways
    and my thoughts above your thoughts. (Is 55:9)

Hail Mary

5 - **NT Meditation**: In the sixth month, the angel Gabriel was sent from God to a town of Galilee called Nazareth, to a virgin betrothed to a man named Joseph, of the house of David, and the virgin's name was Mary. (Lk 1:26-27)

5 - **OT Meditation**: Therefore the Lord himself will give you this sign: the virgin shall be with child, and bear a son, . . . (Is 7:14a)

Hail Mary

6 - **NT Meditation**: And coming to her, he said, "Hail, favored one! The Lord is with you." But she was greatly troubled at what was said and pondered what sort of greeting this might be. (Lk 1:28-29)

6 - **OT Meditation**: . . . "Blessed are you, daughter, by the Most High God, above all the women on earth; . . ." (Jdt 13:18a)

Hail Mary

7 - **NT Meditation**: Then the angel said to her, "Do not be afraid, Mary, for you have found favor with God. Behold, you will conceive in your womb and bear a son, and you shall name him Jesus." (Lk 1:30-31)

7 - **OT Meditation:**
　　Fear not, you shall not be put to shame;
　　　　you need not blush, for you shall not be disgraced.
　　. . . and shall name him Immanuel. (Is 54:4a; Is 7:14b)

Hail Mary

8 - **NT Meditation**: He will be great and will be called Son of the Most High, and the Lord God will give him the throne of David his father, (Lk 1:32)

8 - **OT Meditation**:

His dominion is vast and forever peaceful,
From David's throne, and over his kingdom,
    which he confirms and sustains
By judgment and justice,
    both now and forever. (Is 9:6)

Hail Mary

9 - **NT Meditation**: ". . . and he will rule over the house of Jacob forever, and of his kingdom there will be no end." But Mary said to the angel, "How can this be, since I have no relations with a man?" (Lk 1:33-34)

9 - **OT Meditation**: In the lifetime of those kings the God of heaven will set up a kingdom that shall never be destroyed . . . it shall break in pieces all these kingdoms and put an end to them, and it shall stand forever. (Dn 2:44)

Hail Mary

10 - **NT Meditation**: And the angel said to her in reply, "The holy Spirit will come upon you, and the power of the Most High will overshadow you. Therefore the child to be born will be called holy, the Son of God." (Lk 1:35)

10 - **OT Meditation:**
> The spirit of the LORD will rush upon you, . . .
> For in her is a spirit
> > intelligent, holy, unique,
>
> Manifold, subtle, agile,
> > clear, unstained, certain,
>
> Not baneful, loving the good, keen,
> > Unhampered, beneficent, kindly,
>
> Firm, secure, tranquil, . . .
> > . . . she produces friends of God and prophets.

(1 Sam 10:6; Wis 7:22b-23b & 7:27b)

The Visitation

Our Father

After speaking of the Church, her origin, mission, and destiny, we can find no better way to conclude than by looking to Mary. In her we contemplate what the Church already is in her mystery on her own "pilgrimage of faith," and what she will be in the homeland at the end of her journey. There, "in the glory of the Most Holy and Undivided Trinity," "in the communion of all the saints,"[13] the church is awaited by the one she venerates as Mother of her Lord and as her own mother.[14]

---

13. Cf. LG 69.
14. *Catechism of the Catholic Church*. Article 972.

Hail Mary

1 - **NT Meditation**: ". . . And behold, Elizabeth, your relative, has also conceived a son in her old age, and this is the sixth month for her who was called barren; for nothing will be impossible for God." (Lk 1:36-37)

1 - **OT Meditation**: Is anything too marvelous for the LORD to do? (Gn 18:14a)

Hail Mary

2 - **NT Meditation**: Mary said, "Behold, I am the handmaid of the Lord. May it be done to me according to your word." Then the angel departed from her. (Lk 1:38)

2 - **OT Meditation**:
Seek the LORD, all you humble of the earth,
    who have observed his law;
Seek justice, seek humility; . . . (Zep 2:3a)

Hail Mary

3 - **NT Meditation**: When Elizabeth heard Mary's greeting, the infant leaped in her womb, and Elizabeth, filled with the holy Spirit, cried out in a loud voice and said, "Most blessed are you among women, and blessed is the fruit of your womb. And how does this happen to me, that the mother of my Lord should come to me?" (Lk 1:41-43)

3 - **OT Meditation**: David feared the LORD that day and said, "How can the ark of the LORD come to me?" (2 Sm 6:9)

Hail Mary

4 - **NT Meditation**: ". . . For at the moment the sound of your greeting reached my ears, the infant in my womb leaped for joy. Blessed are you who believed that what was spoken to you by the Lord would be fulfilled." (Lk 1:44-45)

4 - **OT Meditation**:
> O LORD, you are my God,
>> I will extol you and praise your name;
> For you have fulfilled your wonderful plans of old,
>> faithful and true. (Is 25:1)

Hail Mary

5 - **NT Meditation**: Mary remained with her about three months and then returned to her home. (Lk 1:56)

5 - **OT Meditation**: The ark of the LORD remained in the house . . . for three months, and the LORD blessed . . . his whole house. (2 Sm 6:11)

Hail Mary

6 - **NT Meditation**: When the time arrived for Elizabeth to have her child she gave birth to a son. . . . When they came on the eighth day to circumcise the child, they were going to call him Zechariah after his father, but his mother said in reply, "No. He will be called John." (Lk 1:57, 59-60)

6 - **OT Meditation**: This is my covenant with you and your descendants after you that you must keep: every male among you shall be circumcised. (Gn 17:10)

Hail Mary

7 - **NT Meditation**: Then Zechariah his father, filled with the holy Spirit, prophesied, saying:

"Blessed be the Lord, the God of Israel,
    for he has visited and brought redemption to his
        people." (Lk 1:67-68)

7 - **OT Meditation**:
You sent deliverance to your people,
    ratified your covenant forever;
    holy and awesome is your name. (Ps 111:9)

Hail Mary

8 - **NT Meditation**:
He has raised up a horn for our salvation
    within the house of David his servant,
even as he promised through the mouth
    of his holy prophets from of old: (Lk 1:69-70)

8 - **OT Meditation**:
But you, my servant Jacob, fear not, says the LORD,
    be not dismayed, O Israel!
Behold, I will deliver you from the far-off land,
    your descendants, from their land of exile;
Jacob shall again find rest,
    shall be tranquil and undisturbed, . . . (Jer 30:10)

Hail Mary

9 - **NT Meditation**:

And you, child, will be called prophet of the Most High,
   for you will go before the Lord to prepare his ways,
   (Lk 1:76)

9 - **OT Meditation**:

Lo, I am sending my messenger
   to prepare the way before me;
And suddenly there will come to the temple
   the LORD whom you seek,
And the messenger of the covenant
      whom you desire. (Mal 3:1)

Hail Mary

10 - **NT Meditation**:

". . . to give his people knowledge of salvation
   through the forgiveness of their sins,
because of the tender mercy of our God . . .
   to shine on those who sit in darkness and death's
      shadow,
   to guide our feet into the path of peace."
      (Lk 1:77 . . . 79)

10 - **OT Meditation**:

Remember this, O Jacob,
   you, O Israel, who are my servant!
I formed you to be a servant to me;
   O Israel, by me you shall never be forgotten:
I have brushed away your offenses like a cloud,
   your sins like a mist;
      return to me, for I have redeemed you. (Is 44:21-22)

The Nativity

Our Father

With the Nicene Creed, we answer by confessing: "For us men and for our salvation he came down from heaven; by the power of the Holy Spirit, he became incarnate of the Virgin Mary, and was made man."[15]

The Word became flesh for us *in order to save us by reconciling us with God*, who "loved us and sent his Son to be the expiation for our sins": "the Father has sent his Son as the Savior of the world," and "he was revealed to take away sins."[16 & 17]

---

15. *Catechism of the Catholic Church*. Article 456.
16. 1 *Jn* 4:10; 4:14; 3:5.
17. *Catechism of the Catholic Church*. Article 457.

Hail Mary

1 - **NT Meditation**: And Joseph too went up from Galilee from the town of Nazareth to Judea, to the city of David that is called Bethlehem, because he was of the house and family of David, to be enrolled with Mary, his betrothed, who was with child. (Lk 2:4-5)

1 - **OT Meditation**:
(Therefore the Lord will give them up, until the time
    when she who is to give birth has borne,
And the rest of his brethren shall return
    to the children of Israel.) (Mi 5:2)

Hail Mary

2 - **NT Meditation**: and she gave birth to her firstborn son. She wrapped him in swaddling clothes and laid him in a manger, because there was no room for them in the inn. (Lk 2:7)

2 - **OT Meditation**:
An ox knows its owner,
    and an ass, its master's manger;
But Israel does not know,
    my people has not understood. (Is 1:3)

Hail Mary

3 - **NT Meditation**: For today in the city of David a savior has been born for you who is Messiah and Lord. (Lk 2:11)

3 - **OT Meditation**:
For a child is born to us, a son is given us;
upon his shoulder dominion rests. (Is 9:5a)

Hail Mary

4 - **NT Meditation**: When the angels went away from them to heaven, the shepherds said to one another, "Let us go, then, to Bethlehem to see this thing that has taken place, which the Lord has made known to us." So they went in haste and found Mary and Joseph, and the infant lying in the manger. When they saw this, they made known the message that had been told them about this child. All who heard it were amazed by what had been told them by the shepherds. (Lk 2:15-18)

4 - **OT Meditation**:
I see him, though not now;
I behold him, though not near:
A star shall advance from Jacob,
and a staff shall rise from Israel, . . . (Nm 24:17a)

Hail Mary

5 - **NT Meditation**: When Jesus was born . . . magi from the east arrived in Jerusalem, saying, "Where is the newborn king of the Jews? We saw his star at its rising and have come to do him homage." When King Herod heard this, he was greatly troubled, and all Jerusalem with him. (Mt 2:1b-3)

5 - **OT Meditation**:
> That abundance may flourish in his days,
>> great bounty, till the moon be no more. (Ps 72:7)

Hail Mary

6 - **NT Meditation**: Assembling all the chief priests and the scribes of the people, he inquired of them where the Messiah was to be born. They said to him, "In Bethlehem of Judea, for thus it has been written through the prophet:

> 'And you, Bethlehem, land of Judah,
>> are by no means least among the rulers of Judah;
> since from you shall come a ruler,
>> who is to shepherd my people Israel.'" (Mt 2:4-6)

6 - **OT Meditation**:
> But you, Bethlehem-Ephrathah,
>> too small to be among the clans of Judah,
> From you shall come forth for me
>> one who is to be ruler in Israel;
> Whose origin is from of old,
>> from ancient times. (Mi 5:1)

Hail Mary

7 - **NT Meditation**: They were overjoyed at seeing the star, and on entering the house they saw the child with Mary his mother. They prostrated themselves and did him homage. Then they opened their treasures and offered him gifts of gold, frankincense, and myrrh. (Mt 2:10-11)

7 - **OT Meditation**:

Kings shall be your foster fathers,
   their princesses your nurses;
Bowing to the ground, they shall worship you
   and lick the dust at your feet.
Then you shall know that I am the LORD,
   and those who hope in me shall never be disappointed.
   (Is 49:23)

Hail Mary

8 - **NT Meditation**: . . . the angel of the Lord appeared to Joseph in a dream and said, "Rise, take the child and his mother, flee to Egypt, and stay there until I tell you. Herod is going to search for the child to destroy him." . . . He stayed there until the death of Herod, that what the Lord had said through the prophet might be fulfilled, "Out of Egypt I called my son." (Mt 2:13, 15)

8 - **OT Meditation**:

When Israel was a child I loved him,
   out of Egypt I called my son. (Hos 11:1)

Hail Mary

9 - **NT Meditation**: When Herod realized that he had been deceived by the magi, he became furious. He ordered the massacre of all the boys in Bethlehem and its vicinity two years old and under, . . . Then was fulfilled what had been said through Jeremiah the prophet:

> "A voice was heard at Ramah,
>   sobbing and loud lamentation;
> Rachel weeping for her children,
>   and she would not be consoled,
>   since they were no more." (Mt 2:16-18)

9 - **OT Meditation**: Thus says the LORD:
   In Ramah is heard the sound of moaning,
      of bitter weeping!
   Rachael mourns her children,
      she refuses to be consoled
      because her children are no more. (Jer 31:15)

Hail Mary

10 - **NT Meditation**: When Herod had died, behold, the angel of the Lord appeared in a dream to Joseph in Egypt and said, "Rise, take the child and his mother and go to the land of Israel, for those who sought the child's life are dead." (Mt 2:19-20)

10 - **OT Meditation**: In Midian the LORD said to Moses, "Go back to Egypt, for all the men who sought your life are dead." (Ex 4:19)

The Presentation

Our Father

Jesus' *circumcision,* on the eighth day after his birth,[18] is the sign of his incorporation into Abraham's descendants, into the people of the covenant. It is the sign of his submission to the Law[19] and his deputation to Israel's worship, in which he will participate throughout his life. This sign prefigures that "circumcision of Christ" which is Baptism.[20 & 21]

---

18. Cf. *Lk* 2:21.
19. Cf. *Gal* 4:4.
20. Cf. *Col* 2:11-13.
21. *Catechism of the Catholic Church*. Article 527.

Hail Mary

1 - **NT Meditation**: When eight days were completed for his circumcision, he was named Jesus, the name given him by the angel before he was conceived in the womb. (Lk 2:21)

1 - **OT Meditation**: Throughout the ages, every male among you, when he is eight days old, shall be circumcised, . . . (Gn 17:12a)

Hail Mary

2 - **NT Meditation**: When the days were completed for their purification according to the law of Moses, they took him up to Jerusalem to present him to the Lord, just as it is written in the law of the Lord, "Every male that opens the womb shall be consecrated to the Lord," (Lk 2:22-23)

2 - **OT Meditation**: "Consecrate to me every first-born that opens the womb among the Israelites, . . . for it belongs to me." (Ex 13:2)

Hail Mary

3 - **NT Meditation**: and to offer the sacrifice of "a pair of turtledoves or two young pigeons," in accordance with the dictate in the law of the Lord. (Lk 2:24)

3 - **OT Meditation**: . . . she may take two turtledoves or two pigeons, the one for a holocaust and the other for a sin offering. (Lv 12:8a)

Hail Mary

4 - **NT Meditation**: Now there was a man in Jerusalem whose name was Simeon. . . . It had been revealed to him by the holy Spirit that he should not see death before he had seen the Messiah of the Lord. (Lk 2:25a;26)

4 - **OT Meditation**:
> Be kind to your servant that I may live,
>> that I may keep your word.
> Open my eyes to see clearly
>> the wonders of your teachings. (Ps 119:17-18)

Hail Mary

5 - **NT Meditation**: He came in the Spirit into the temple; and when the parents brought in the child Jesus to perform the custom of the law in regard to him, he took him into his arms and blessed God, saying: (Lk 2:27-28)

5 - **OT Meditation**:
> The LORD has bared his holy arm
>> in the sight of all the nations;
> All the ends of the earth will behold
>> the salvation of our God. (Is 52:10)

Hail Mary

6 - **NT Meditation**:
"Now, Master, you may let your servant go
    in peace, according to your word,
for my eyes have seen your salvation,
    which you prepared in the sight of all the peoples,
a light for revelation to the Gentiles,
    and glory for your people Israel." (Lk 2:29-32)

6 - **OT Meditation**:
I am bringing on my justice, it is not far off,
    my salvation shall not tarry;
I will put salvation within Zion,
    and give to Israel my glory. (Is 46:13)

Hail Mary

7 - **NT Meditation**: The child's father and mother were
amazed at what was said about him; and Simeon blessed
them and said to Mary his mother, "Behold, this child is
destined for the fall and rise of many in Israel, and to be a
sign that will be contradicted (and you yourself a sword will
pierce) so that the thoughts of many hearts may be revealed."
(Lk 2:33-35)

7 - **OT Meditation**:
I will make you a light to the nations,
    that my salvation may reach to the ends of the earth.
    (Is 49:6b)

Hail Mary

8 - **NT Meditation**: He went and dwelt in a town called Nazareth, so that what had been spoken through the prophets might be fulfilled, "He shall be called a Nazorean." (Mt 2:23)

8 – **OT Meditation:**
". . . On with the plan of the Holy One of Israel!
let it come to pass, that we may know it!" (Is 5:19b)

Hail Mary

9- **NT Meditation**: And coming forward at that very time, she gave thanks to God and spoke about the child to all who were awaiting the redemption of Jerusalem. (Lk 2:38)

9 - **OT Meditation**:
See, my servant shall prosper,
he shall be raised high and greatly exalted. (Is 52:13)

Hail Mary

10 - **NT Meditation**: The child grew and became strong, filled with wisdom; and the favor of God was upon him. (Lk 2:40)

10 - **OT Meditation**:
The spirit of the LORD shall rest upon him:
a spirit of wisdom and of understanding,
A spirit of counsel and of strength,
a spirit of knowledge and of fear of the LORD,
and his delight shall be the fear of the LORD. (Is 11:2-3)

The Finding of Our Lord in the Temple

Our Father

Like the prophets before him Jesus expressed the deepest respect for the Temple in Jerusalem. It was in the Temple that Joseph and Mary presented him forty days after his birth.[22] At the age of twelve he decided to remain in the Temple to remind his parents that he must be about his Father's business.[23 & 24]

---

22. Cf. *Lk* 2:22-39.
23. Cf. *Lk* 2:46-49.
24. *Catechism of the Catholic Church*. Article 583.

Hail Mary

1 - **NT Meditation**: Each year his parents went to Jerusalem for the feast of Passover, and when he was twelve years old, they went up according to festival custom. (Lk 2:41-42)

1 - **OT Meditation**: You shall keep the feast of Unleavened Bread. As I have commanded you, you must eat unleavened bread for seven days at the prescribed time in the month . . . for it was then that you came out of Egypt . . . (Ex 23:15)

Hail Mary

2 - **NT Meditation**: After they had completed its days, as they were returning, the boy Jesus remained behind in Jerusalem, but his parents did not know it. (Lk 2:43)

2 - **OT Meditation**:
I raise my eyes toward the mountains.
    From where will my help come?
My help comes from the LORD,
    the maker of heaven and earth. (Ps 121:1-2)

Hail Mary

3 - **NT Meditation**: Thinking that he was in the caravan, they journeyed for a day and looked for him among their relatives and acquaintances, (Lk 2:44)

3 - **OT Meditation**:

The LORD is your guardian;
    the LORD is your shade
    at your right hand.
By day the sun cannot harm you,
    nor the moon by night. (Ps 121:5-6)

Hail Mary

4 - **NT Meditation**: but not finding him, they returned to Jerusalem to look for him. (Lk 2:45)

4 - **OT Meditation**:

The LORD will guard you from all evil,
    will always guard your life.
The LORD will guard your coming and going
    both now and forever. (Ps 121:7-8)

Hail Mary

5 - **NT Meditation**: After three days they found him in the temple, sitting in the midst of the teachers, listening to them and asking them questions, (Lk 2:46)

5 - **OT Meditation**:

Attend, my people, to my teaching;
    listen to the words of my mouth. (Ps 78:1)

Hail Mary

6 - **NT Meditation**: and all who heard him were astounded at his understanding and his answers. (Lk 2:47)

6 - **OT Meditation**:
I will open my mouth in story,
    drawing lessons from of old. (Ps 78:2)

Hail Mary

7 - **NT Meditation**: When his parents saw him, they were astonished, and his mother said to him, "Son, why have you done this to us? Your father and I have been looking for you with great anxiety." (Lk 2:48)

7 - **OT Meditation**:
At all times my soul is stirred
    with longing for your edicts. (Ps 119:20)

Hail Mary

8- **NT Meditation**: And he said to them, "Why were you looking for me? Did you not know that I must be in my Father's house?" But they did not understand what he said to them. (Lk 2:49-50)

8 - **OT Meditation**:
Because zeal for your house consumes me, (Ps 69:10a)

Hail Mary

9 - **NT Meditation**: He went down with them and came to Nazareth, and was obedient to them; and his mother kept all these things in her heart. (Lk 2:51)

9 - **OT Meditation**:
A wise son makes his father glad, (Prv 10:1a)

Hail Mary

10 - **NT Meditation**: And Jesus advanced [in] wisdom and age and favor before God and man. (Lk 2:52)

10 - **OT Meditation**:
Receive my instruction in preference to silver,
and knowledge rather than choice gold.
[For Wisdom is better than corals,
and no choice possession can compare with her.]
(Prv 8:10-11)

The
Luminous
Mysteries

The Baptism in the Jordan

Our Father

The baptism of Jesus is on his part the acceptance and inauguration of his mission as God's suffering Servant. He allows himself to be numbered among sinners; he is already "the Lamb of God, who takes away the sin of the world."[25] . . . At his baptism "the heavens were opened"[26] – the heavens that Adam's sin had closed – and the waters were sanctified by the descent of Jesus and the Spirit, a prelude to the new creation.[27]

---

25. Cf. *Jn* 1:29; cf. *Isa* 53:12.
26. Cf. *Mt* 3:16.
27. *Catechism of the Catholic Church*. Article 536.

Hail Mary

1 - **NT Meditation**: The beginning of the gospel of Jesus Christ [the Son of God]. As it is written in Isaiah the prophet:

"Behold, I am sending my messenger ahead of you;
  he will prepare your way.
A voice of one crying out in the desert:
  'Prepare the way of the Lord,
  make straight his paths.' " (Mk 1:1-3)

1 - **OT Meditation**: A voice cries out:
  In the desert prepare the way of the LORD!
  Make straight in the wasteland a
    highway for our God! (Is 40:3)

Hail Mary

2 - **NT Meditation**: John [the] Baptist appeared in the desert proclaiming a baptism of repentance for the forgiveness of sins. . . . And this is what he proclaimed: "One mightier than I is coming after me. I am not worthy to stoop and loosen the thongs of his sandals. (Mk 1:4, 7)

2 - **OT Meditation**: God said, "Come no nearer! Remove the sandals from your feet, for the place where you stand is holy ground. . . ." (Ex 3:5)

Hail Mary

3 - **NT Meditation**: People of the whole Judean countryside and all the inhabitants of Jerusalem were going out to him and were being baptized by him in the Jordan River as they acknowledged their sins. ". . . I have baptized you with water; he will baptize you with the holy Spirit."
(Mk 1:5, 8)

3 - **OT Meditation**:
I will bring the one third through fire,
and I will refine them as silver is refined,
and I will test them as gold is tested. (Zec 13:9)

Hail Mary

4 - **NT Meditation**: ". . . His winnowing fan is in his hand. He will clear his threshing floor and gather his wheat into his barn, but the chaff he will burn with unquenchable fire."
(Mt 3:12)

4 - **OT Meditation**:
I winnowed them with the fan
in every city gate.
I destroyed my people through bereavement;
they returned not from their evil ways. (Jer 15:7)

Hail Mary

5 - **NT Meditation**: Then Jesus came from Galilee to John at the Jordan to be baptized by him . . . On coming up out of the water he saw the heavens being torn open and the Spirit, like a dove, descending upon him. (Mt 3:13; Mk 1:10)

5 - **OT Meditation**: The king stood up, rent his garments, and then lay on the ground. All his servants standing by him also rent their garments. (2 Sm 13:31)

Hail Mary

6 - **NT Meditation**: And a voice came from the heavens, saying, "This is my beloved Son, with whom I am well pleased." (Mt 3:17)

6 - **OT Meditation**:
Here is my servant whom I uphold,
my chosen one with whom I am pleased,
Upon whom I have put my spirit;
he shall bring forth justice to the nations, (Is 42:1)

Hail Mary

7 - **NT Meditation**: Then Jesus was led by the Spirit into the desert to be tempted by the devil. He fasted for forty days and forty nights, and afterwards he was hungry. (Mt 4:1-2)

7 - **OT Meditation**: But Moses passed into the midst of the cloud as he went up on the mountain; and there he stayed for forty days and forty nights. (Ex 24:18)

Hail Mary

8 - NT Meditation: The tempter approached and said to him, "If you are the Son of God, command that these stones become loaves of bread." He said in reply, "It is written: . . ." (Mt 4:3-4a)

8 - OT Meditation: . . . not by bread alone does man live, but by every word that comes forth from the mouth of the LORD. (Dt 8:3b)

Hail Mary

9 - NT Meditation: Then the devil took him to the holy city, and made him stand on the parapet of the temple, and said to him, "If you are the Son of God, throw yourself down. For it is written:

'He will command his angels concerning you,'
    and 'with their hands they will support you,
lest you dash your foot against a stone.'"

Jesus answered him, . . . (Mt 4:5-7a)

9 - OT Meditation: "You shall not put the LORD, your God, to the test, . . . (Dt 6:16)

Hail Mary

10 - **NT Meditation**: Then the devil took him up to a very high mountain, and showed him all the kingdoms of the world in their magnificence, and he said to him, "All these I shall give to you, if you will prostrate yourself and worship me." At this, Jesus said to him, "Get away, Satan! It is written: . . ." (Mt 4:8-10a)

10 - **OT Meditation**: The LORD, your God, shall you fear; him shall you serve, and by his name shall you swear. (Dt 6:13)

The Miracle at Cana

Our Father

The Gospel reveals to us how Mary prays and intercedes in faith. At Cana,[28] the mother of Jesus asks her son for the needs of a wedding feast; this is the sign of another feast – that of the wedding of the Lamb where he gives his body and blood at the request of the Church, his Bride. It is at the hour of the New Covenant, at the foot of the cross,[29] that Mary is heard as the Woman, the new Eve, the true "Mother of all the living."[30]

---

28. Cf. *Jn* 2:1-12.
29. Cf. *Jn* 19:25-27.
30. *Catechism of the Catholic Church.* Article 2618.

Hail Mary

1 - **NT Meditation**: On the third day there was a wedding in Cana in Galilee, and the mother of Jesus was there. Jesus and his disciples were also invited to the wedding. (Jn 2:1-2)

1 - **OT Meditation**: "The sons . . . are celebrating a great wedding, and with a large escort they are bringing the bride, . . ." "That is my master," replied the servant. Then she covered herself with her veil. (1 Mc 9:37b; Gn 24:65b)

Hail Mary

2 - **NT Meditation:** When the wine ran short, the mother of Jesus said to him, "They have no wine." (Jn 2:3)

2 - **OT Meditation**:
   My vineyard is at my own disposal; (Song 8:12a)

Hail Mary

3 - **NT Meditation:** [And] Jesus said to her, "Woman, how does your concern affect me? My hour has not yet come." (Jn 2:4)

3 - **OT Meditation**: But the king replied: "What business is it of mine or of yours . . ." (2 Sm 16:10a)

Hail Mary

4 - **NT Meditation**: His mother said to the servers, "Do whatever he tells you." (Jn 2:5)

4 - **OT Meditation**: . . . Pharaoh directed all the Egyptians to go to Joseph and do whatever he told them. (Gn 41:55b)

Hail Mary

5 - **NT Meditation**: Now there were six stone water jars there for Jewish ceremonial washings, each holding twenty to thirty gallons. (Jn 2:6)

5 - **OT Meditation**: When they are about to enter the meeting tent, they must wash with water, lest they die. (Ex 30:20a)

Hail Mary

6 - **NT Meditation**: Jesus told them, "Fill the jars with water." So they filled them to the brim. (Jn 2:7)

6 - **OT Meditation**:
   Then will your barns be filled with grain,
      with new wine your vats will overflow. (Prv 3:10)

Hail Mary

7 - **NT Meditation**: Then he told them, "Draw some out now and take it to the headwaiter." So they took it. (Jn 2:8)

7 - **OT Meditation**:

  Yes, the days are coming,
    says the LORD, . . .
    they shall . . .
  Plant vineyards and drink the wine,
    set out gardens and eat the fruits. (Am 9:13a, 14b, c)

Hail Mary

8 - **NT Meditation**: And when the headwaiter tasted the water that had become wine, without knowing where it came from (although the servers who had drawn the water knew), . . . (Jn 2:9a-b)

8 - **OT Meditation**:

  With harp and lyre, timbrel and flute,
    they feast on wine; (Is 5:12a)

Hail Mary

9 - **NT Meditation**: . . . the headwaiter called the bridegroom and said to him, "Everyone serves good wine first, and then when people have drunk freely, an inferior one; but you have kept the good wine until now." (Jn 2:9b-10)

9 - **OT Meditation**:

  Let us have our fill of costly wine . . . (Wis 2:7a)

Hail Mary

10 - **NT Meditation**: Jesus did this as the beginning of his signs in Cana in Galilee and so revealed his glory, and his disciples began to believe in him. (Jn 2:11)

10 - **OT Meditation**:
Blessed be the LORD, the God of Israel,
who alone does wonderful deeds. (Ps 72:18)

The Proclamation of the Kingdom of God

Our Father

Everyone is called to enter the kingdom. First announced to the children of Israel, this messianic kingdom is intended to accept men of all nations.[31] To enter it, one must first accept Jesus' word . . .[32]

The kingdom belongs *to the poor and lowly*, which means those who have accepted it with humble hearts. Jesus is sent to "preach good news to the poor";[33] he declares them blessed, for "theirs is the kingdom of heaven."[34 & 35]

---

31. Cf. *Mt* 8:11; 10:5-7; 28:19.
32. *Catechism of the Catholic Church*. Article 543.
33. Cf. *Lk* 4:18; cf. 7:22.
34. *Mt* 5:3.
35. *Catechism of the Catholic Church*. Article 544.

Hail Mary

1 - **NT Meditation**: "This is the time of fulfillment. The kingdom of God is at hand. Repent, and believe in the gospel." (Mk 1:15)

1 - **OT Meditation**: Samuel said to them: "If you wish with your whole heart to return to the LORD, put away your foreign gods and . . . devote yourselves to the LORD, and worship him alone. Then he will deliver you . . ." (1 Sm 7:3a)

Hail Mary

2 - **NT Meditation**: Then they came to Capernaum, and on the sabbath he entered the synagogue and taught. The people were astonished at his teaching, for he taught them as one having authority and not as the scribes. (Mk 1:21-22)

2 - **OT Meditation**:
He gives wisdom to the wise
and knowledge to those who understand. (Dn 2:21b)

Hail Mary

3 - **NT Meditation**: When he saw the crowds, he went up the mountain . . . He began to teach them, saying:

"Blessed are the poor in spirit,
for theirs is the kingdom of heaven. . . ." (Mt 5:1a, 2-3)

3 - **OT Meditation**:
The lowly will ever find joy in the LORD,
and the poor rejoice in the Holy One
of Israel. (Is 29:19)

Hail Mary

4 – NT **Meditation**:
Blessed are they who mourn,
for they will be comforted. (Mt 5:4)

4 - **OT Meditation**:
Those who sow in tears
will reap with cries of joy. (Ps 126:5)

Hail Mary

5 - NT Meditation:
Blessed are the meek,
    for they will inherit the land. (Mt 5:5)

5 - OT Meditation:
For the upright will dwell in the land,
    the honest will remain in it; (Prv 2:21)

Hail Mary

6 - NT Meditation:
Blessed are they who hunger and thirst for righteousness,
    for they will be satisfied. (Mt 5:6)

6 - OT Meditation:
He who pursues justice and kindness
    will find life and honor. (Prv 21:21)

Hail Mary

7 - NT Meditation:
Blessed are the clean of heart,
    for they will see God. (Mt 5:8)

7 - OT Meditation:
The LORD loves the pure of heart; (Prv 22:11a)

Hail Mary

8 - **NT Meditation**: Your heavenly Father knows that you need them all. But seek first the kingdom [of God] and his righteousness, and all these things will be given you besides. (Mt 6:32b-33)

8 - **OT Meditation**:
Love justice, you who judge the earth;
  think of the LORD in goodness,
  and seek him in integrity of heart; (Wis 1:1)

Hail Mary

9 - **NT Meditation**: "Everyone who listens to these words of mine and acts on them will be like a wise man who built his house on rock. . . ." (Mt 7:24)

9 - **OT Meditation**:
When the tempest passes, the wicked man is no more;
  but the just man is established forever. (Prv 10:25)

Hail Mary

10 - **NT Meditation**: He heard this and said, "Those who are well do not need a physician, but the sick do. Go and learn the meaning of the words, 'I desire mercy, not sacrifice.' I did not come to call the righteous but sinners." (Mt 9:12-13)

10 - **OT Meditation**:
For it is love that I desire, not sacrifice,
  and knowledge of God rather than holocausts.
  (Hos 6:6)

The Transfiguration

Our Father

For a moment Jesus discloses his divine glory, confirming
Peter's confession. He also reveals that he will have to go by
the way of the cross at Jerusalem in order to "enter into his
glory."[36] Moses and Elijah had seen God's glory on the
Mountain; the Law and the Prophets had announced the
Messiah's sufferings.[37] . . . the cloud indicates the presence
of the Holy Spirit. "The whole Trinity appeared: the Father
in the voice; the Son in the man; the Spirit in the shining
cloud."[38 & 39]

---

36. Cf. *Lk* 24:26.
37. Cf. *Lk* 24:27.
38. Cf. St. Thomas Aquinas, *STh* III, 45, 4, *ad* 2.
39. *Catechism of the Catholic Church*. Article 555.

Hail Mary

1 - **NT Meditation**: When Jesus went into the region . . . he asked his disciples, "Who do people say that the Son of Man is?" (Mt 16:13)

1 - **OT Meditation**:
  . . . I saw
    One like a son of man coming,
      on the clouds of heaven; (Dn 7:13a)

Hail Mary

2 - **NT Meditation**: Simon Peter said in reply, "You are the Messiah, the Son of the living God." (Mt 16:16)

2 - **OT Meditation**:
  "For he is the living God, enduring forever;
    his kingdom shall not be destroyed,
    and his dominion shall be without end . . ." (Dn 6:27b)

Hail Mary

3 - **NT Meditation**: And so I say to you, you are Peter, and upon this rock I will build my church, and the gates of the netherworld shall not prevail against it. (Mt 16:18)

3 - **OT Meditation**:
> He shall cry to me, 'You are my father,
>> my God, the Rock that brings me victory!'
> I myself make him firstborn,
>> Most High over the kings of the earth. (Ps 89:27-28)

Hail Mary

4 - **NT Meditation**:
> I will give you the keys to the kingdom of heaven.
>> (Mt 16:19a)

4 - **OT Meditation**:
> I will place the key of the House of
>> David on his shoulder; (Is 22:22a)

Hail Mary

5 - **NT Meditation**: ". . . Whatever you bind on earth shall be bound in heaven; and whatever you loose on earth shall be loosed in heaven." (Mt 16:19b)

5 - **OT Meditation**:
> when he opens, no one shall shut,
> when he shuts, no one shall open. (Is 22:22b)

Hail Mary

6 - **NT Meditation**: For the Son of Man will come with his angels in his Father's glory, and then he will repay everyone according to his conduct. (Mt 16:27)

6 - **OT Meditation**:
  Rather, he requites men for their conduct,
    and brings home to a man his way of life. (Jb 34:11)

Hail Mary

7 - **NT Meditation**: After six days Jesus took Peter, James, and John his brother, and led them up a high mountain by themselves. (Mt 17:1)

7 - **OT Meditation**: The glory of the LORD settled upon Mount Sinai. The cloud covered it for six days, . . . (Ex 24:16a)

Hail Mary

8 - **NT Meditation**: And he was transfigured before them; his face shone like the sun and his clothes became white as light. (Mt 17:2)

8 - **OT Meditation**: As Moses came down from Mount Sinai with the two tablets of the commandments in his hands, he did not know that the skin of his face had become radiant while he conversed with the LORD. (Ex 34:29)

Hail Mary

9 - **NT Meditation:** While he was still speaking, behold, a bright cloud cast a shadow over them, then from the cloud came a voice that said, "This is my beloved Son, with whom I am well pleased; listen to him." (Mt 17:5)

9 - **OT Meditation**:
    . . . "You are my son;
       today I am your father. . . ." (Ps 2:7b)

Hail Mary

10 - **NT Meditation**: When the disciples heard this, they fell prostrate and were very much afraid. (Mt 17:6)

10 - **OT Meditation**: Then Joshua fell prostrate to the ground in worship, . . . (Jos 5:14b)

The Institution of the Eucharist

Our Father

The Lord, having loved those who were his own, loved them to the end. Knowing that the hour had come to leave this world and return to the Father, in the course of a meal he washed their feet and gave them the commandment of love.[40] In order to leave them a pledge of this love, in order never to depart from his own and to make them sharers in his Passover, he instituted the Eucharist as the memorial of his death and Resurrection, and commanded his apostles to celebrate it until his return; "thereby he constituted them priests of the New Testament."[41 & 42]

---

40. Cf. *Jn* 13:1-17; 34-35.
41. Council of Trent (1562): DS 1740.
42. *Catechism of the Catholic Church*. Article 1337.

Hail Mary

1 - **NT Meditation**: Jesus said to them, "I am the bread of life; whoever comes to me will never hunger, and whoever believes in me will never thirst. . . ." (Jn 6:35)

1 - **OT Meditation**:
> All you who are thirsty,
>> come to the water!
> You who have no money,
>> come, receive grain and eat; (Is 55:1a)

Hail Mary

2 - **NT Meditation**: No one can come to me unless the Father who sent me draw him, and I will raise him on the last day. It is written in the prophets:
'They shall be taught by God.' (Jn 6:44-45a)

2 - **OT Meditation**:
> All your sons shall be taught by the LORD,
>> and great shall be the peace of your children. (Is 54:13)

Hail Mary

3 - **NT Meditation**: I am the bread of life. Your ancestors ate the manna in the desert, but they died; this is the bread that comes down from heaven so that one may eat it and not die. (Jn 6:48-50)

3 - **OT Meditation**:
> You gave food to those who fear you,
>> mindful of your covenant forever. (Ps 111:5)

Hail Mary

4 - **NT Meditation:** For my flesh is true food, and my blood is true drink. Whoever eats my flesh and drinks my blood remains in me and I in him. (Jn 6:55-56)

4 - **OT Meditation**:
    Forsake foolishness that you may live;
        advance in the way of understanding.
    For by me your days will be multiplied
        and the years of your life increased. (Prv 9:6; 11)

Hail Mary

5 - **NT Meditation**: While they were eating, Jesus took bread, said the blessing, broke it, and giving it to his disciples said, . . . (Mt 26:26a)

5 - **OT Meditation**: Melchizedek, king of Salem, brought out bread and wine, . . . he blessed Abram . . .
    The LORD has sworn and he will not waver:
        "Like Melchizedek you are a priest forever."
    (Gn 14:18a . . . Ps 110:4)

Hail Mary

6 - **NT Meditation**: "Take and eat; this is my body."
(Mt 26:26b)

6 - **OT Meditation**:

> Instead of this, you nourished your people with food of
> angels
>> and furnished them bread from heaven, ready to hand,
>> untoiled-for,
>> endowed with all delights and conforming to every
>> taste. (Wis 16:20)

Hail Mary

7 - **NT Meditation**: Then he took a cup, gave thanks, and
gave it to them saying, . . . (Mt 26:27a)

7 - **OT Meditation**:

> I will raise the cup of salvation
>> and call on the name of the LORD. (Ps 116:13)

Hail Mary

8 - **NT Meditation**: "Drink from it, all of you . . ."
(Mt 26:27b)

8 - **OT Meditation**:

> Come, eat of my food,
>> and drink of the wine I have mixed! (Prv 9:5)

Hail Mary

9 - **NT Meditation**: for this is my blood of the covenant, which will be shed on behalf of many for the forgiveness of sins. (Mt 26:28)

9 - **OT Meditation**:
  Come to me heedfully,
    listen, that you may have life.
  I will renew with you the everlasting covenant,
    the benefits assured to David. (Is 55:3)

Hail Mary

10 - **NT Meditation**: Then, after singing a hymn, they went out to the Mount of Olives. (Mt 26:30)

10 - **OT Meditation**:
  Come, let us sing joyfully to the LORD;
    cry out to the rock of our salvation. (Ps 95:1)

The Sorrowful Mysteries

The Agony of Our Lord in the Garden

Our Father

The cup of the New Covenant, which Jesus anticipated when he offered himself at the Last Supper, is afterwards accepted by him from his Father's hand in his agony in the garden at Gethsemani,[43] making himself "obedient unto death." . . . By accepting in his human will that the Father's will be done, he accepts his death as redemptive, for "he himself bore our sins in his body on the tree."[44] & [45]

---

43. Cf. *Mt* 26:42; *Lk* 22:20.
44. Cf. *1 Pet* 2:24; cf. *Mt* 26:42.
45. *Catechism of the Catholic Church*. Article 612.

Hail Mary

1 - **NT Meditation**: Then they came to a place named Gethsemane, and he said to his disciples, "Sit here while I pray." He took with him Peter, James, and John, . . . (Mk 14:32-33a)

1 - **OT Meditation**:
Grant me justice, LORD!
I have walked without blame.
In the LORD I have trusted;
I have not faltered. (Ps 26:1-2)

Hail Mary

2 - **NT Meditation**: . . . and began to be troubled and distressed. Then he said to them, "My soul is sorrowful even to death. Remain here and keep watch." (Mk. 14:33b-34)

2 - **OT Meditation**:
Do not stay far from me,
for trouble is near,
and there is no one to help. (Ps 22:12)

Hail Mary

3 - **NT Meditation**: He advanced a little and fell to the ground and prayed that if it were possible the hour might pass by him; (Mk 14:35)

3 - **OT Meditation**:
Rescue me from my enemies, my God;
   lift me out of reach of my foes.
Deliver me from evildoers;
   from the bloodthirsty save me. (Ps 59:2-3)

Hail Mary

4 - **NT Meditation**: he said, "Abba, Father, all things are possible to you. Take this cup away from me, but not what I will but what you will." (Mk 14:36)

4 - **OT Meditation**:
LORD, my allotted portion and my cup,
   you have made my destiny secure. (Ps 16:5)

Hail Mary

5 - **NT Meditation**: When he returned he found them asleep. He said to Peter, "Simon, are you asleep? Could you not keep watch for one hour? . . ." (Mk 14:37)

5 - **OT Meditation**:
On you I depend since birth;
   from my mother's womb you are my strength;
   my hope in you never wavers. (Ps 71:6)

Hail Mary

6 - **NT Meditation**: ". . . Watch and pray that you may not undergo the test. The spirit is willing but the flesh is weak." (Mk 14:38)

6 - **OT Meditation**:
O Most High, when I am afraid,
    in you I place my trust.
God, I praise your promise;
    in you I trust, I do not fear.
    What can mere flesh do to me? (Ps 56:3b-5)

Hail Mary

7 - **NT Meditation**: Withdrawing again, he prayed, saying the same thing. (Mk 14:39)

7 - **OT Meditation**:
This I know: God is on my side.
God, I praise your promise;
    in you I trust, I do not fear.
    What can mere mortals do to me? (Ps 56:10b-12)

Hail Mary

8- **NT Meditation**: Then he returned once more and found them asleep, for they could not keep their eyes open and did not know what to answer him. (Mk 14:40)

8 - OT Meditation:

Hear my cry, O God,
    listen to my prayer!
From the brink of Sheol I call;
    my heart grows faint.
Raise me up, set me on a rock,
    for you are my refuge,
        a tower of strength against the foe. (Ps 61:2-4)

Hail Mary

9 - **NT Meditation**: He returned a third time and said to them, "Are you still sleeping and taking your rest? It is enough. The hour has come. Behold, the Son of Man is to be handed over to sinners. . . ." (Mk 14:41)

9 - OT Meditation:

Deliver me, LORD, from the wicked;
    preserve me from the violent,
From those who plan evil in their hearts,
    who stir up conflicts every day, (Ps 140:2-3)

Hail Mary

10 - **NT Meditation**: ". . . Get up, let us go. See, my betrayer is at hand." (Mk 14:42)

10 - **OT Meditation**:
> Wounds from a friend may be accepted as well meant,
>> but the greetings of an enemy one
>> prays against. (Prv 27:6)

The Scourging at the Pillar

Our Father

In her Magisterial teaching of the faith and in the witness of her saints, the Church has never forgotten that "sinners were the authors and the ministers of all the sufferings that the divine Redeemer endured."[46 & 47]

---

46. *Roman Catechism* I,5,11; cf.*Heb* 12:3.
47. *Catechism of the Catholic Church*. Article 598.

Hail Mary

1 - **NT Meditation**: Those who had arrested Jesus led him away to Caiaphas the high priest, where the scribes and the elders were assembled. (Mt 26:57)

1 - **OT Meditation**: "I am completely trapped," . . . "If I yield, it will be my death; if I refuse, I cannot escape your power. Yet it is better for me to fall into your power without guilt than to sin before the Lord." (Dn 13:22-23)

Hail Mary

2 - **NT Meditation**: The chief priests and the entire Sanhedrin kept trying to obtain false testimony against Jesus . . . but they found none, though many false witnesses came forward. (Mt 26:59-60)

2 - **OT Meditation**:
　　You love evil rather than good,
　　　　lies rather than honest speech.
　　You love any word that destroys,
　　　　you deceitful tongue. (Ps 52:5-6)

Hail Mary

3 - **NT Meditation**: When day came the council of elders of the people met, both chief priests and scribes, and they brought him before their Sanhedrin. They said, "If you are the Messiah, tell us," but he replied to them, "If I tell you, you will not believe, and if I question, you will not respond. . . ." (Lk 22:66-68)

3 - **OT Meditation**:
Let us beset the just one, because he is obnoxious to us;
    he sets himself against our doings,
Reproaches us for transgressions of the law
    and charges us with violations of our training.
    (Wis 2:12)

Hail Mary

4 - **NT Meditation**: ". . . But from this time on the Son of Man will be seated at the right hand of the power of God." (Lk 22:69)

4 - **OT Meditation**:
As I watched,
Thrones were set up
    and the Ancient One took his throne.
His clothing was snow bright,
    and the hair on his head as white as wool; . . .
Thousands upon thousands were ministering to him,
    and myriads upon myriads attended him.
    (Dn 7:9a, 10b)

Hail Mary

5 - **NT Meditation**: They all asked, "Are you then the Son of God?" He replied to them, "You say that I am." Then they said, "What further need have we for testimony? We have heard it from his own mouth." (Lk 22:70-71)

5 - **OT Meditation**:
> He professes to have knowledge of God
> > and styles himself a child of the LORD. (Wis 2:13)

Hail Mary

6 - **NT Meditation**: As soon as morning came, the chief priests with the elders and the scribes, that is, the whole Sanhedrin, held a council. They bound Jesus, led him away, and handed him over to Pilate. (Mk 15:1)

6 - **OT Meditation**:
> Commit your way to the LORD;
> > trust that God will act
> And make your integrity shine like the dawn,
> > your vindication like noonday. (Ps 37:5-6)

Hail Mary

7 - **NT Meditation**: They brought charges against him, saying, "We found this man misleading our people; he opposes the payment of taxes to Caesar and maintains that he is the Messiah, a king." (Lk 23:2)

7 - **OT Meditation**:
> Be not a witness against your neighbor without just cause,
> > thus committing folly with your lips. (Prv 24:28)

Hail Mary

8 - **NT Meditation**: Pilate questioned him, "Are you the king of the Jews?" He said to him in reply, "You say so." The chief priests accused him of many things. Again Pilate questioned him, "Have you no answer? See how many things they accuse you of." Jesus gave him no further answer, so that Pilate was amazed. (Mk 15:2-5)

8 - **OT Meditation**:
> I have set my face like flint,
> > knowing that I shall not be put to shame. (Is 50:7b)

Hail Mary

9 - **NT Meditation**: Pilate again said to them in reply, "Then what [do you want] me to do with [the man you call] the king of the Jews?" They shouted again, "Crucify him." Pilate said to them, "Why? What evil has he done?" They only shouted the louder, "Crucify him." (Mk 15:12-13)

9 - **OT Meditation**:
Hear me, you who know justice,
    you people who have my teaching at heart:
Fear not the reproach of men,
    be not dismayed at their revilings. (Is 51:7)

Hail Mary

10 - **NT Meditation**: Then he released Barabbas to them, but after he had Jesus scourged, he handed him over to be crucified. (Mt. 27:26)

10- **OT Meditation**:
The oppressed shall soon be released;
    they shall not die and go down into the pit,
    nor shall they want for bread. (Is 51:14)

The Crowning with Thorns

Our Father

After agreeing to baptize him along with the sinners, John the Baptist looked at Jesus and pointed him out as the "Lamb of God, who takes away the sin of the world."[48] By doing so, he reveals that Jesus is at the same time the suffering Servant who silently allows himself to be led to the slaughter and who bears the sin of the multitudes, and also the Paschal Lamb, the symbol of Israel's redemption at the first Passover.[49 & 50]

---

48. *Jn* 1:29; cf. *Lk* 3:21; *Mt* 3:14-15; *Jn* 1:36.
49. *Isa* 53:7, 12; cf. *Jer* 11:19; *Ex* 12:3-14; *Jn* 19:36; *1 Cor* 5:7.
50. *Catechism of the Catholic Church*. Article 608.

Hail Mary

1 - **NT Meditation**: Weaving a crown out of thorns, they placed it on his head, and a reed in his right hand. . . . They spat upon him and took the reed and kept striking him on the head. (Mt 27:29a; 30)

1 - **OT Meditation**:
My face I did not shield
    from buffets and spitting. (Is 50:6b)

Hail Mary

2 - **NT Meditation**: and they came to him and said, "Hail, King of the Jews!" And they struck him repeatedly. (Jn 19:3)

2 - **OT Meditation**:
I gave my back to those who beat me,
    my cheeks to those who plucked my beard; (Is 50:6a)

Hail Mary

3 - **NT Meditation**: Once more Pilate went out and said to them, "Look, I am bringing him out to you, so that you may know that I find no guilt in him." (Jn 19:4)

3 - **OT Meditation**:
Though he was harshly treated, he submitted
    and opened not his mouth; (Is 53:7a)

Hail Mary

4 - NT Meditation: So Jesus came out, wearing the crown of thorns and the purple cloak. And he said to them, "Behold, the man!" (Jn 19:5)

4 - OT Meditation:
   In you, LORD, I take refuge;
      let me never be put to shame. (Ps 71:1)

Hail Mary

5 - NT Meditation: When the chief priests and the guards saw him they cried out, "Crucify him, crucify him!" Pilate said to them, "Take him yourselves and crucify him. I find no guilt in him." (Jn 19:6)

5 - OT Meditation:
   Yet it was our infirmities that he bore,
      our sufferings that he endured,
   While we thought of him as stricken,
      as one smitten by God and afflicted. (Is 53:4)

Hail Mary

6 - NT Meditation: The Jews answered, "We have a law, and according to that law he ought to die, because he made himself the Son of God." (Jn 19:7)

6 - OT Meditation:
   . . . he was cut off from the land of the living,
      and smitten for the sin of his people, (Is 53:8b)

Hail Mary

7 - **NT Meditation**: . . . Pilate . . . went back into the praetorium and said to Jesus, "Where are you from?" Jesus did not answer him. (Jn 19:8a; 9)

7 - **OT Meditation**:
　Like a lamb led to the slaughter
　　or a sheep before the shearers,
　　he was silent and opened not his mouth. (Is 53:7b)

Hail Mary

8 - **NT Meditation:** So Pilate said to him, "Do you not speak to me? Do you not know that I have power to release you and I have power to crucify you?" (Jn 19:10)

8 - **OT Meditation:**
　You are my hope, Lord;
　　my trust, GOD, from my youth. (Ps 71:5)

Hail Mary

9 - **NT Meditation**: Jesus answered [him], "You would have no power over me if it had not been given to you from above. For this reason the one who handed me over to you has the greater sin." (Jn 19:11)

9 - **OT Meditation**:
　The LORD is my light and my salvation;
　　whom do I fear?
　The LORD is my life's refuge;
　　of whom am I afraid? (Ps 27:1)

Hail Mary

10 - **NT Meditation**: And he said to the Jews, "Behold, your king!" They cried out, "Take him away, take him away! Crucify him!" (Jn 19:14b-15a)

10 - **OT Meditation**:
  LORD, grant victory to the king;
    answer when we call upon you. (Ps 20:10)

The Carrying of the Cross

Our Father

The cross is the unique sacrifice of Christ, the "one mediator between God and men."[51] . . . He calls his disciples to "take up [their] cross and follow [him],"[52] for "Christ also suffered for [us] leaving [us] an example so that [we] should follow in his steps."[53 & 54]

---

51. *1 Tim* 2:5.
52. *Mt* 16:24.
53. *1 Pet* 2:21.
54. *Catechism of the Catholic Church*. Article 618.

Hail Mary

1 - **NT Meditation**: Then he said to all, "If anyone wishes to come after me, he must deny himself and take up his cross daily and follow me. . . ." (Lk 9:23)

1 - **OT Meditation**:

Let him who is wise understand these things;
    let him who is prudent know them.
Straight are the paths of the LORD,
    in them the just walk,
    but sinners stumble in them. (Hos 14:10)

Hail Mary

2 - **NT Meditation**: and carrying the cross himself he went out to what is called the Place of the Skull, in Hebrew, Golgotha. (Jn 19:17)

2 - **OT Meditation**:

Oppressed and condemned, he was taken away,
    and who would have thought any more of his destiny?
    (Is 53:8a)

Hail Mary

3 - **NT Meditation**: As they led him away they took hold of a certain Simon, a Cyrenian, who was coming in from the country; and after laying the cross on him, they made him carry it behind Jesus. (Lk 23:26)

3 - **OT Meditation**:
He was spurned and avoided by men,
    a man of suffering, accustomed to infirmity.
One of those from whom men hid their faces,
    spurned, and we held him in no esteem. (Is 53:3)

Hail Mary

4 - **NT Meditation**: "Come to me, all you who labor and are burdened, and I will give you rest. . . ." (Mt 11:28)

4 - **OT Meditation**:
Through his suffering, my servant shall justify many,
    and their guilt he shall bear. (Is 53:11b)

Hail Mary

5 - **NT Meditation**: ". . . Take my yoke upon you and learn from me, for I am meek and humble of heart; and you will find rest for yourselves. For my yoke is easy, and my burden light." (Mt 11:29-30)

5 - **OT Meditation**:
> [But the LORD was pleased
>   to crush him in infirmity.]
>
> If he gives his life as an offering for sin,
>   he shall see his descendants in a long life,
>   and the will of the LORD shall be accomplished
>   through him. (Is 53:10)

Hail Mary

6 - **NT Meditation**: A large crowd of people followed Jesus, including many women who mourned and lamented him. (Lk 23:27)

6 - **OT Meditation**:
> We had all gone astray like sheep,
>   each following his own way;
> But the LORD laid upon him
>   the guilt of us all. (Is 53:6)

Hail Mary

7 - **NT Meditation**: Jesus turned to them and said, "Daughters of Jerusalem, do not weep for me; weep instead for yourselves and for your children, . . ." (Lk 23:28)

7 - **OT Meditation**: . . . and I saw sitting there the women who were weeping . . . he said . . . Do you see this, son of man? You shall see other abominations, greater than these! (Ez 8:14b-15)

Hail Mary

8 - **NT Meditation**: ". . .for indeed, the days are coming when people will say, 'Blessed are the barren, the wombs that never bore and the breasts that never nursed.'. . ." (Lk 23:29)

8 - **OT Meditation**:
Raise a glad cry, you barren one who did not bear,
 break forth in jubilant song, you who were not in
  labor, . . . (Is 54:1a)

Hail Mary

9 - **NT Meditation**: ". . . At that time people will say to the mountains, 'Fall upon us!' and to the hills, 'Cover us!' for if these things are done when the wood is green what will happen when it is dry?" (Lk 23:30-31)

9 - **OT Meditation**:

Then they shall cry out to the mountains, "Cover us!"
and to the hills, "Fall upon us!" (Hos 10:8b)

Hail Mary

10- **NT Meditation**: They brought him to the place of Golgotha (which is translated Place of the Skull). They gave him wine drugged with myrrh, but he did not take it. (Mk 15:22-23)

10 - **OT Meditation**:

Along the way I walk
they have hidden a trap for me.
I look to my right hand,
but no friend is there.
There is no escape for me;
no one cares for me. (Ps 142:4b-5)

The Crucifixion

Our Father

It is love "to the end"[55] that confers on Christ's sacrifice its value as redemption and reparation, as atonement and satisfaction. He knew and loved us all when he offered his life.[56] . . . No man, not even the holiest, was ever able to take on himself the sins of all men and offer himself as a sacrifice for all.[57]

---

55. *Jn* 13:1.
56. Cf. *Gal* 2:20; *Eph* 5:2, 25.
57. *Catechism of the Catholic Church*. Article 616.

Hail Mary

1 - **NT Meditation**: Now two others, both criminals, were led away with him to be executed. . . . Now one of the criminals hanging there reviled Jesus, . . . The other, however, rebuking him, said in reply, . . . "Jesus, remember me when you come into your kingdom." He replied to him, "Amen, I say to you, today you will be with me in Paradise." (Lk 23:32, 39a, 40a, 42a-43)

1 - **OT Meditation**:

Because he surrendered himself to death
and was counted among the wicked;
And he shall take away the sins of many,
and win pardon for their offenses.

. . . Answer them: As I live, says the Lord GOD, I swear I take no pleasure in the death of the wicked man, but rather in the wicked man's conversion, that he may live. Turn, turn from your evil ways! Why should you die, O house of Israel? (Is 53:12b; Ez 33:11)

Hail Mary

2 - **NT Meditation**: Those passing by reviled him, shaking their heads and saying, "You who would destroy the temple and rebuild it in three days, save yourself, if you are the Son of God, [and] come down from the cross!" (Mt 27:39-40)

2 - **OT Meditation**:

All who see me mock me;
   they curl their lips and jeer;
   they shake their heads at me:
"You relied on the LORD—let him deliver you;
   if he loves you, let him rescue you." (Ps 22: 8-9)

Hail Mary

3 - **NT Meditation**: And about three o'clock Jesus cried out in a loud voice, "*Eli, Eli, lema sabachthani*?" which means, "My God, my God, why have you forsaken me?" Some of the bystanders who heard it said, "This one is calling for Elijah." (Mt 27:46-47)

3 - **OT Meditation**:

My God, my God, why have you abandoned me?
   Why so far from my call for help,
   from my cries of anguish? (Ps 22:2)

Hail Mary

4 - **NT Meditation**: When the soldiers had crucified Jesus, they took his clothes and divided them into four shares, a share for each soldier. They also took his tunic, but the tunic was seamless, woven in one piece from the top down. So they said to one another, "Let's not tear it, but cast lots for it to see whose it will be," in order that the passage of scripture might be fulfilled [that says]: . . .

> "They divided my garments among them,
>   and for my vesture they cast lots." (Jn 19:23-24)

4 - **OT Meditation**:
> they divide my garments among them;
>   for my clothing they cast lots. (Ps 22:19)

Hail Mary

5 - **NT Meditation**: After this, aware that everything was now finished, in order the scripture might be fulfilled, Jesus said, "I thirst." There was a vessel filled with common wine. So they put a sponge soaked in wine on a sprig of hyssop and put it up to his mouth. When Jesus had taken the wine, he said, "It is finished." And bowing his head, he handed over the spirit. (Jn 19:28-30)

5 - **OT Meditation**:
> As dry as a potsherd is my throat;
>   my tongue sticks to my palate; . . .
> I wait for you, O LORD;
>   I lift up my soul to my God.
> In you I trust; do not let me be disgraced;
>   do not let my enemies gloat over me.
>   (Ps 22:16a; 25:1-2)

Hail Mary

6 - **NT Meditation**: But when they came to Jesus and saw that he was already dead, they did not break his legs, (Jn 19:33)

6 - **OT Meditation**:
  So wasted are my hands and feet
    that I can count all my bones. (Ps 22:17b-18a)

Hail Mary

7 - **NT Meditation**: but one soldier thrust his lance into his side, and immediately blood and water flowed out. (Jn 19:34)

7 - **OT Meditation**: I will pour out on the house of David and on the inhabitants of Jerusalem a spirit of grace and petition; (Zec 12:10a)

Hail Mary

8 - **NT Meditation**: For this happened so that the scripture passage might be fulfilled:

"Not a bone of it will be broken." (Jn 19:36)

8 - **OT Meditation**:
  God watches over all their bones;
    not a one shall be broken. (Ps 34:21)

Hail Mary

9 - **NT Meditation**: And again another passage says:

"They will look upon him whom they
    have pierced." (Jn 19:37)

9 - **OT Meditation**: . . . and they shall look on him whom
they have thrust through, and they shall mourn for him as
one mourns for an only son, and they shall grieve over him
as one grieves over a first-born. (Zec 12:10b)

Hail Mary

10 - **NT Meditation**: Taking the body, Joseph wrapped it
[in] clean linen and laid it in his new tomb that he had hewn
in the rock. (Mt 27:59-60)

10 - **OT Meditation**:
    A grave was assigned him among the wicked
        and a burial place with evildoers,
    Though he had done no wrong
        nor spoken any falsehood. (Is 53:9)

The
Glorious
Mysteries

The Resurrection

Our Father

The Father's power "raised up" Christ his Son and by doing so perfectly introduced his Son's humanity, including his body, into the Trinity. Jesus is conclusively revealed as "Son of God in power according to the Spirit of holiness by his Resurrection from the dead."[58 & 59]

---

58. *Rom* 1:3-4; cf. *Acts* 2:24.
59. *Catechism of the Catholic Church*. Article 648.

Hail Mary

1 - **NT Meditation**: So she ran and went to Simon Peter and to the other disciple whom Jesus loved, and told them, "They have taken the Lord from the tomb, and we don't know where they put him." (Jn 20:2)

1 - **OT Meditation**: Therefore, prophesy and say to them: Thus says the Lord GOD: O my people, I will open your graves and have you rise from them, and bring you back to the land of Israel. . . . thus you shall know that I am the LORD, I have promised, and I will do it, says the LORD. (Ez 37:12, 14b)

Hail Mary

2 - **NT Meditation**: Then the other disciple also went in, the one who had arrived at the tomb first, and he saw and believed. (Jn 20:8)

2 - **OT Meditation**:
   He will revive us after two days;
      on the third day he will raise us up,
      to live in his presence. (Hos 6:2)

Hail Mary

3 - **NT Meditation**: Jesus said to her, "Woman, why are you weeping? Whom are you are looking for?" She thought it was the gardener and said to him, "Sir, if you carried him away, tell me where you laid him, and I will take him." Jesus said to her, "Mary!" She turned and said to him in Hebrew, "Rabbouni," which means Teacher. (Jn 20:15-16)

3 - **OT Meditation**:
> But as for me, I know that my Vindicator lives,
> (Jb 19:25a)

Hail Mary

4 - **NT Meditation**: Jesus said to her, "Stop holding on to me, for I have not yet ascended to the Father. But go to my brothers and tell them, 'I am going to my Father and your Father, to my God and your God.'" (Jn 20:17)

4 - **OT Meditation**: But Ruth said, "Do not ask me to abandon or forsake you! for wherever you go I will go, wherever you lodge I will lodge, your people shall be my people, and your God my God. (Ru 1:16)

Hail Mary

5 - **NT Meditation**: And when he had said this, he breathed on them and said to them, "Receive the holy Spirit. Whose sins you forgive are forgiven them, and whose sins you retain are retained." (Jn 20:22-23)

5 - **OT Meditation**: the LORD God formed man out of the clay of the ground and blew into his nostrils the breath of life, and so man became a living being. (Gn 2:7)

Hail Mary

6 - **NT Meditation**: Thomas answered and said to him, "My Lord and my God!" Jesus said to him, "Have you come to believe because you have seen me? Blessed are those who have not seen and have believed." (Jn 20:28-29)

6 - **OT Meditation**:
   Awake, be vigilant in my defense,
      in my cause, my God and my Lord. (Ps 35:23)

Hail Mary

7 - **NT Meditation**: ". . . But you will receive power when the holy Spirit comes upon you, and you will be my witnesses in Jerusalem, throughout Judea and Samaria, and to the ends of the earth." (Acts 1:8)

7 - **OT Meditation**:
You are my witnesses, says the LORD,
    my servants whom I have chosen
To know and believe in me
    and understand that it is I.
Before me no god was formed,
    and after me there shall be none. (Is 43:10)

Hail Mary

8 - **NT Meditation**: When he had said this, as they were looking on, he was lifted up, and a cloud took him from their sight. (Acts 1:9)

8 - **OT Meditation**: As they walked on conversing, a flaming chariot and flaming horses came between them, and Elijah went up to heaven in a whirlwind. (2 Kgs 2:11)

Hail Mary

9 - **NT Meditation**: For if the dead are not raised, neither has Christ been raised, and if Christ has not been raised, your faith is vain; you are still in your sins.
(1 Cor 15:16-17)

9 - **OT Meditation**: Thus says the Lord GOD: From the four winds come, O spirit, and breathe into these slain that they may come to life. (Ez 37:9b)

Hail Mary

10 - **NT Meditation**: And when this which is corruptible clothes itself with incorruptibility and this which is mortal clothes itself with immortality, then the word that is written shall come about:

"Death is swallowed up in victory.
Where, O death, is your victory?
Where, O death, is your sting?" (1 Cor 15:54-55)

10 - **OT Meditation**:
Shall I deliver them from the power of the nether world?
    shall I redeem them from death?
Where are your plagues, O death!
    where is your sting, O nether world! (Hos 13:14a)

The Ascension

Our Father

" 'No one has ascended into heaven but he who descended from heaven, the Son of man.'[60] Left to its own natural powers humanity does not have access to the "Father's house," to God's life and happiness.[61] Only Christ can open to man such access that we, his members, might have confidence that we too shall go where he, our Head and our Source, has preceded us."[62 & 63]

---

60. *Jn* 3:13; cf. *Eph* 4:8-10.
61. *Jn* 14:2.
62. *Roman Missal*, Preface of the Ascension: *"sed ut illuc confideremus, sua membra, nos subsequi quo ipse, caput nostrum principiumque, praecessit."*
63. *Catechism of the Catholic Church*. Article 661.

Hail Mary

1 - **NT Meditation**: So you also are now in anguish. But I will see you again, and your hearts will rejoice, and no one will take your joy away from you. (Jn 16:22)

1 - **OT Meditation**:
   Those who go forth weeping,
      carrying sacks of seed,
   Will return with cries of joy,
      carrying their bundled sheaves. (Ps 126:6)

Hail Mary

2 - **NT Meditation**: But God raised him up, releasing him from the throes of death, because it was impossible for him to be held by it. For David says of him:

   'I saw the Lord ever before me, . . .' (Acts 2:24-25a)

2 - **OT Meditation**:
   I keep the LORD always before me; (Ps 16:8a)

Hail Mary

3 - **NT Meditation**:
   . . . with him at my right hand I shall not be disturbed.
   (Acts 2:25b)

3 - **OT Meditation:**
   . . . with the Lord at my right, I shall never be shaken.
   (Ps 16:8b)

Hail Mary

4 - **NT Meditation**:
Therefore my heart has been glad and my tongue has exulted; (Acts 2:26a)

4 - **OT Meditation**:
Therefore my heart is glad, my soul rejoices. (Ps 16:9a)

Hail Mary

5 - **NT Meditation**:
. . . my flesh, too, will dwell in hope, (Acts 2:26b)

5 - **OT Meditation**:
. . . my body also dwells secure, (Ps 16:9b)

Hail Mary

6 - **NT Meditation**:
. . . because you will not abandon my soul
to the netherworld, (Acts 2:27a)

6 - **OT Meditation**:
For you will not abandon me to Sheol, (Ps 16:10a)

Hail Mary

7 - **NT Meditation**:
. . . nor will you suffer your holy one to see corruption. (Acts 2:27b)

7 - **OT Meditation**:
. . . nor let your faithful servant see the pit. (Ps 16:10b)

Hail Mary

8 - NT Meditation:
You have made known to me the paths of life;
(Acts 2:28a)

8 - OT Meditation:
You will show me the path to life, (Ps 16:11a)

Hail Mary

9 - NT Meditation:
'. . . you will fill me with joy in your presence.'
(Acts 2:28b)

9 - OT Meditation:
. . . abounding joy in your presence,
the delights at your right hand forever. (Ps 16:11b)

Hail Mary

10 - **NT Meditation**: For David did not go up into heaven, but he himself said:

'The Lord said to my Lord,
"Sit at my right hand
until I make your enemies your foot stool.' "
(Acts 2:34-35)

10 - **OT Meditation**:
The LORD says to you, my lord:

"Take your throne at my right hand,
while I make your enemies your foot stool." (Ps 110:1)

The Descent of the Holy Spirit
Upon the Apostles

Our Father

On the day of Pentecost, the Spirit of the Promise was poured out on the disciples, gathered "together in one place."[64] While awaiting the Spirit, "all these with one accord devoted themselves to prayer."[65] The Spirit who teaches the Church and recalls for her everything that Jesus said[66] was also to form her in the life of prayer.[67]

---

64. *Acts* 2:1.
65. *Acts* 1:14.
66. Cf. *Jn* 14:26.
67. *Catechism of the Catholic Church*. Article 2623.

Hail Mary

1 - **NT Meditation**: When the time for Pentecost was fulfilled, they were all in one place together. (Acts 2:1)

1 - **OT Meditation**: "You shall keep the feast of Weeks . . ." (Ex 34:22a)

Hail Mary

2 - **NT Meditation**: And suddenly there came from the sky a noise like a strong driving wind, and it filled the entire house in which they were. (Acts 2:2)

2 - **OT Meditation**: when suddenly a great wind came across the desert and smote the four corners of the house. (Jb 1:19a)

Hail Mary

3 - **NT Meditation**: Then there appeared to them tongues as of fire, which parted and came to rest on each one of them. (Acts 2:3)

3 - **OT Meditation**: Mount Sinai was all wrapped in smoke, for the LORD came down upon it in fire. (Ex 19:18a)

Hail Mary

4 - **NT Meditation**: And they were all filled with the holy Spirit and began to speak in different tongues, as the Spirit enabled them to proclaim. (Acts 2:4)

4 - **OT Meditation**:
When you send forth your breath, they are created,
     and you renew the face of the earth. (Ps 104:30)

Hail Mary

5 - **NT Meditation**: They were astounded, and in amazement they asked, "Are not all these people who are speaking Galileans? Then how does each of us hear them in his own native language? . . ." (Acts 2:7-8)

5 - **OT Meditation**:
For the spirit of the LORD fills the world,
     is all-embracing, and knows what man says. (Wis 1:7)

Hail Mary

6 - **NT Meditation**:
"'It will come to pass in the last days,' God says,
     'that I will pour out a portion of my spirit upon all
          flesh. . . .' " (Acts 2:17a)

6 - **OT Meditation**:
I will pour out my spirit upon your offspring,
     and my blessing upon your descendants. (Is 44:3b)

Hail Mary

7 - **NT Meditation**:

Your sons and daughters shall prophesy,
   your young men shall see visions,
   your old men shall dream dreams. (Acts 2:17b)

7 - **OT Meditation**:

Your sons and daughters shall prophesy,
   your old men shall dream dreams,
   your young men shall see visions; (Jl 3:1b)

Hail Mary

8 - **NT Meditation**:

Indeed, upon my servants and my handmaids
   I will pour out a portion of my spirit in those days,
      and they shall prophesy. (Acts 2:18)

8 - **OT Meditation**:

Even upon the servants and the handmaids,
   in those days, I will pour out my spirit. (Jl 3:2)

Hail Mary

9 - **NT Meditation**:

And I will work wonders in the heavens above
   and signs on the earth below:
      blood, fire, and a cloud of smoke. (Acts 2:19)

9 - **OT Meditation**:

And I will work wonders in the heavens and on the earth,
   blood, fire, and columns of smoke; (Jl 3:3)

Hail Mary

10 - NT Meditation:

'. . . and it shall be that everyone shall be saved who calls on the name of the Lord.' (Acts 2:21)

10 - OT Meditation:

Then everyone shall be rescued
    who calls on the name of the LORD; (Jl 3:5a)

The Assumption of Mary into Heaven

Our Father

The Most Blessed Virgin Mary, when the course of her earthly life was completed, was taken up body and soul into the glory of heaven, where she already shares in the glory of her Son's Resurrection, anticipating the resurrection of all members of his Body.[68]

---

68. *Catechism of the Catholic Church*. Article 974.

Hail Mary

1 - **NT Meditation**: And Mary said:
"My soul proclaims the greatness of the Lord; . . ." (Lk 1:46)

1 - **OT Meditation**:
"My heart exults in the LORD, . . .
There is no Holy One like the LORD;
    there is no Rock like our God. (1 Sm 2:1a; 2)

Hail Mary

2 - **NT Meditation**:
my spirit rejoices in God my savior. (Lk 1:47)

2 - **OT Meditation**:
I rejoice heartily in the LORD,
    in my God is the joy of my soul; (Is 61:10a)

Hail Mary

3 - **NT Meditation**:
For he has looked upon his handmaid's lowliness;
    behold, from now on will all ages call me blessed.
    (Lk 1:48)

3 - **OT Meditation**:
For he has clothed me with a robe of salvation,
    and wrapped me in a mantle of justice, (Is 61:10b)

Hail Mary

4 - **NT Meditation**:
   The Mighty One has done great things for me,
      and holy is his name. (Lk 1:49)

4 - **OT Meditation**:
   Your redeemer is the Holy One of Israel,
      called God of all the earth. (Is 54:5b)

Hail Mary

5 - **NT Meditation**:
   His mercy is from age to age
      to those who fear him. (Lk 1:50)

5 - **OT Meditation**:
   But the LORD's kindness is forever,
      toward the faithful from age to age. (Ps 103:17a)

Hail Mary

6 - **NT Meditation**:
   He has shown might with his arm,
      dispersed the arrogant of mind and heart. (Lk 1:51)

6 - **OT Meditation**:
   He frustrates the plans of the cunning,
      so that their hands achieve no success; (Jb 5:12)

Hail Mary

7 - **NT Meditation**:

He has thrown down the rulers from their thrones
but lifted up the lowly. (Lk 1:52)

7 - **OT Meditation**:

For judgment comes not from east or from west,
not from the desert or from the mountains,
But from God who decides,
who brings some low and raises others high.
(Ps 75:7-8)

Hail Mary

8 - **NT Meditation**:

The hungry he has filled with good things;
the rich he has sent away empty. (Lk 1:53)

8 - **OT Meditation**:

For he satisfied the thirsty,
filled the hungry with good things. (Ps 107:9)

Hail Mary

9 - **NT Meditation**:

He has helped Israel his servant,
remembering his mercy, (Lk 1:54)

9 - **OT Meditation**:

He has remembered faithful love
toward the house of Israel. (Ps 98:3a)

Hail Mary

10 - **NT Meditation**:
". . . according to his promise to our fathers,
to Abraham and to his descendants forever." (Lk 1:55)

10 - **OT Meditation**: ". . . and in your descendants all the
nations of the earth shall find blessing - all this because you
obeyed my command." (Gn 22:18)

The Coronation of Mary

Our Father

"Finally the Immaculate Virgin, preserved free from all stain of original sin, when the course of her earthly life was finished, was taken up body and soul into heavenly glory, and exalted by the Lord as Queen over all things, so that she might be the more fully conformed to her Son, the Lord of lords and conqueror of sin and death."[69 & 70]

---

69. *LG* 59; cf. Pius XII, *Munificentissimus Deus* (1950): DS 3903; cf. *Rev* 19:16.
70. *Catechism of the Catholic Church*. Article 966.

Hail Mary

1 - **NT Meditation**: . . . Christ loved the church and handed himself over for her to sanctify her, cleansing her by the bath of water with the word, that he might present to himself the church in splendor, without spot or wrinkle or any such thing, that she might be holy and without blemish. (Eph 5:25-27)

1 - **OT Meditation**:
You are all-beautiful, my beloved,
    and there is no blemish in you. (Song 4:7)

Hail Mary

2 - **NT Meditation**:
Then God's temple in heaven was opened, . . .
(Rv. 11:19a . . .)

2 - **OT Meditation**:
Thus in the chosen city he has given me rest,
    in Jerusalem is my domain. (Sir 24:11)

Hail Mary

3 - **NT Meditation**: . . . and the ark of his covenant could be seen in the temple. (Rv 11:19a)

3 - **OT Meditation**:
Like a star shining among the clouds,
    like the full moon at the holyday season;
Like the sun shining upon the temple,
    like the rainbow appearing in the cloudy sky;
    (Sir 50:6-7)

Hail Mary

4 - **NT Meditation**: There were flashes of lightning, rumblings, and peals of thunder, an earthquake, and a violent hailstorm. (Rv. 11:19b)

4 - **OT Meditation**: He said to me: This gate is to remain closed; it is not to be opened for anyone to enter by it; since the LORD, the God of Israel, has entered by it, it shall remain closed. (Ez 44:2)

Hail Mary

5 - **NT Meditation**: A great sign appeared in the sky, a woman clothed with the sun, with the moon under her feet, and on her head a crown of twelve stars. (Rv. 12:1)

5 - **OT Meditation**:
Who is this that comes forth like the dawn,
     as beautiful as the moon, as resplendent as the sun,
     as awe-inspiring as bannered troops? (Song 6:10)

Hail Mary

6 - **NT Meditation**: She gave birth to a son, a male child, destined to rule all nations with an iron rod. Her child was caught up to God and his throne. (Rv 12:5)

6 - **OT Meditation**: Then he sat down upon his throne, and a throne was provided for the king's mother, who sat at his right. (1 Kgs 2:19b)

Hail Mary

7 - **NT Meditation**: The serpent, however, spewed a torrent of water out of his mouth after the woman to sweep her away with the current. (Rv 12:15)

7 - **OT Meditation**:
Deep waters can not quench love,
   nor floods sweep it away. (Song 8:7a)

Hail Mary

8 - **NT Meditation**: But the earth helped the woman and opened its mouth and swallowed the flood that the dragon spewed out of its mouth. (Rv 12:16)

8 - **OT Meditation**:
For stern as death is love,
   relentless as the nether world is devotion; (Song 8:6b)

Hail Mary

9 – **NT Meditation**: I also saw the holy city, a new Jerusalem, coming down out of heaven from God, prepared as a bride adorned for her husband. (Rv 21:2)

9 - **OT Meditation**:
All glorious is the king's daughter as she enters,
   her raiment threaded with gold;
In embroidered apparel she is led to the king.
The maids of her train are presented to the king.
(Ps 45:14-15)

Hail Mary

10 - **NT Meditation**: I heard a loud voice from the throne saying, "Behold, God's dwelling is with the human race. He will dwell with them and they will be his people and God himself will always be with them [as their God]. He will wipe every tear from their eyes, and there shall be no more death or mourning, wailing or pain, [for] the old order has passed away." (Rv 21:3-4)

10 - **OT Meditation**:
". . . For he who finds me finds life,
    and wins favor from the LORD;
But he who misses me harms himself;
    all who hate me love death." (Prv 8:35-36)

Gentlemen:

Please send me _____ (copies) of **THE NARRATIVE ROSARY**.

Name _____

Address _____

City _____

State _____

Zip _____

Enclosed is my payment of _____ in US Dollars Only!
Please add $5.00 S/H in USA per copy.
Please add $9.00 for International mailing per copy.
Indiana residents, please add 6% Sales Tax.
Additional copies can be purchased by calling
(574) 772-2335
Sorry, no Credit Cards, foreign checks or monies are accepted.
All payment must be made in US Funds

Mail payment to:
CHARLES M. URBAN, SR.
8690 E. Long Lane Drive
Knox, IN 46534 (USA)